WORLD WAR 1 BATTLESHIP

Richard Humble

Illustrated by
Doug Harker

Franklin Watts
London · New York · Toronto · Sydney

© Franklin Watts 1989

Franklin Watts
96 Leonard Street
London EC2A 4RH

First published in the USA by
Franklin Watts Inc.
387 Park Avenue South
New York
N.Y. 10016

First published in Australia by
Franklin Watts Australia
14 Mars Road
Lane Cove
NSW 2066

UK edition ISBN: 0 86313 908 6
US edition ISBN: 0-531-10739-6
Library of Congress Catalog Card
No: 89-5818

Designer: Ben White
Illustrations: Doug Harker
Maps: Hayward Art Group

Photographs: Imperial War
Museum 4, 5, 6, 7, 9t, 10, 11, 13,
20, 27, 29; Hulton Picture Library
9b; "Ullstein" 22; By courtesy of the
Orkney Library – Photographics
Archive 28/29

Typeset by Lineage Ltd,
Watford, England

Printed in Belgium

Words in bold appear in the glossary.

Contents

Battle Fleet at Sea!

For over 350 years, the world's most powerful warship type remained the wooden sailing battleship. There was very little real difference between the *Mary Rose* of King Henry VIII (1545) and Horatio Nelson's *Victory*, which was launched in 1765 and served with the British Fleet for 70 years. Both fought with **broadsides** of cannon arranged on several gun-decks, firing through square holes cut in the sides of the ship.

Over the 50 years after the *Victory*'s last year of service (1835), battleships changed completely. Steam engines replaced sails after the Industrial Revolution. Exploding shells replaced solid iron cannonballs. Iron hulls replaced wood; and the need for **armour-plate** protection against enemy shellfire made the battleship a steel-clad floating fortress. The old broadsides were replaced by pairs of much heavier guns mounted in armoured **turrets**, which could be turned from side to side without the need to turn the whole ship.

These new guns could hit their targets at far greater distances than in the "age of sail". Fleets of sailing battleships fought by battering each other at ranges of 50 metres (160 ft) or less. By the outbreak of World War I in 1914, a battleship's guns could hurl their huge shells 15 kilometres (9 miles) or more.

At the Battle of Trafalgar in 1805, 27 British sailing battleships had beaten 33 from France and Spain. But any single battleship from the fleets that went to war in 1914 could have blown all 60 of the Trafalgar ships out of the water without suffering a scratch.

▷ A battle fleet of 1914 was made up of 3/4 battle **squadrons,** each of 6-8 battleships. The battle squadrons cruised side by side when searching for the enemy, but were trained to form a single "line of battle" — offering the big guns the maximum number of targets — when the enemy fleet was sighted. Radio was still crude in 1914, and flags were still used to pass orders from ship to ship.

▷ One squadron had a special role: the **battle-cruiser** squadron. In 1914, battle-cruisers were a new type of heavy warship. Armed with battleship-sized guns, they were bigger and much faster than battleships, but lacking the heavy armour of the true battleship. The job of the battle-cruisers was to use their speed to cruise ahead of the main battle fleet, seek out the enemy fleet, and lure it within range of the battle fleet's deadly line of heavy guns.

The "All big-gun" ship

During the gradual transformation of the battleship between 1850 and 1900, the British had taken the lead. To cope with as many different types of enemy ship as possible, British ship designers added a growing range of turret guns in a wide range of calibres (the size of a gun measured by the width of its shell).

By 1904 the newest class of British battleship had 12-inch (30.5cm), 9.2-inch (23cm) and 6-inch (15cm) guns. Similar ships were being built by other leading sea powers: France, Russia, the United States, and especially Germany. The German Emperor, Wilhelm II, was jealous of Britain's world empire and was determined to build a navy strong enough to match that of Britain.

The head of the British Navy, Admiral Lord Fisher, was determined to beat off the growing German challenge. He ordered an entirely new type of battleship: the **Dreadnought** –

△ Britain's HMS *Devastation,* the first turret-gun battleship built entirely without masts and sails, under way in 1873. Her best possible speed was 10 knots in good weather but *Dreadnought,* 32 years later, could make 21 knots.

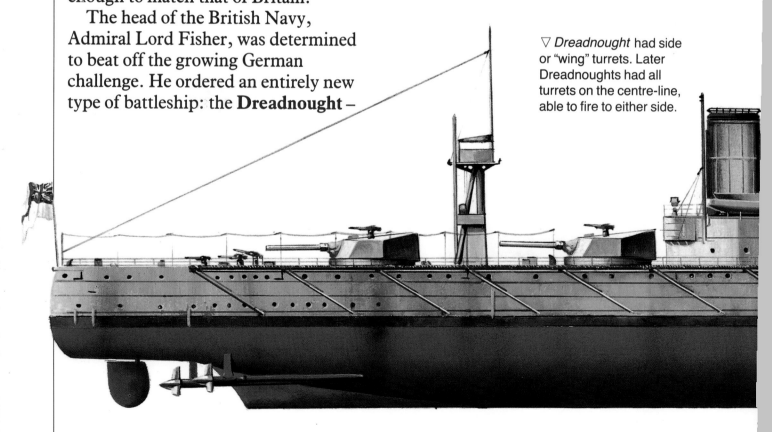

▽ *Dreadnought* had side or "wing" turrets. Later Dreadnoughts had all turrets on the centre-line, able to fire to either side.

6

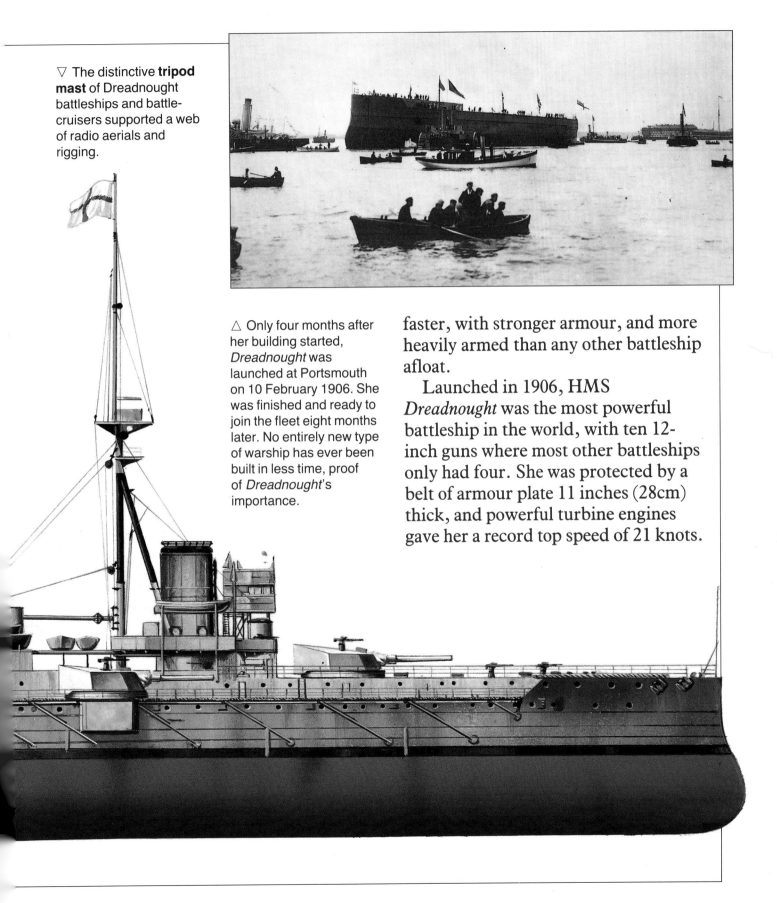

▽ The distinctive **tripod mast** of Dreadnought battleships and battle-cruisers supported a web of radio aerials and rigging.

△ Only four months after her building started, *Dreadnought* was launched at Portsmouth on 10 February 1906. She was finished and ready to join the fleet eight months later. No entirely new type of warship has ever been built in less time, proof of *Dreadnought*'s importance.

faster, with stronger armour, and more heavily armed than any other battleship afloat.

Launched in 1906, HMS *Dreadnought* was the most powerful battleship in the world, with ten 12-inch guns where most other battleships only had four. She was protected by a belt of armour plate 11 inches (28cm) thick, and powerful turbine engines gave her a record top speed of 21 knots.

Life on board

The original complement or crew of HMS *Dreadnought* was 773 officers and men, but as Dreadnought-type battleships were built ever bigger and more powerful up to and during World War I, so complements increased. HMS *Agincourt*, Britain's most powerful Dreadnought in 1914-15 (fourteen 12-inch guns in seven turrets) had a complement of 1,115.

A Dreadnought's crew was basically divided between the stokers who kept the engines going and the seamen who kept the ship in top condition and manned the guns in battle. When the fleet was lying at anchor, daily life in a

△ Looking after the big guns after target practice at sea. The huge barrels of a Dreadnought's rearmost turret are lowered in order to have their linings scoured and cleaned by a team of "gun sweepers".

△ The endless round of scraping and painting. The wear and tear of life at sea meant that a battleship's crew always had some job of "rust chipping" to do. Here teams are suspended on cradles repainting a funnel.

◁ Meal-time for sailors in a later Dreadnought, *Royal Oak,* built in 1914-16. The vertical lines support the mess-deck tables. Apart from electric bulbs, extra light is provided by the round **scuttles** in the ship's sides (closed with armoured **deadlights** when in heavy seas or going into battle).

Dreadnought was an endless round of cleaning, polishing, painting, inspections, and training drills. Many sailors preferred life in smaller ships, where the daily routine was more relaxed than in a battleship.

Every sailor belonged to a living area or "mess", and life off-duty was lived on the **mess-deck**. Here the men rigged tables for eating and slung their hammocks for sleeping. If battleship life had one great advantage, it was that the men had far more living space than in smaller ships like cruisers or destroyers.

Before joining a battleship's crew new sailors underwent a tough training, on training ships and at shore stations, in the basics of seamanship and gunnery, to prepare them for life at sea.

▷ A petty officer; the two stripes on his sleeve indicate that he has between 8 to 12 years' good conduct.

◁ Sailors were trained to be able to fight on land if landing forces were needed. These are trainee sailors undergoing rifle or "musketry" drill in a British training ship.

Coaling by manpower

There was one part of Dreadnought life that all the crew shared, and it was the filthiest job of all. This was the process known as "coaling ship", or filling the bunkers below the waterline with the ship's main fuel.

Though the battleships of World War I represented the most advanced technology of the age, their steam-producing furnaces were still fired by coal. The fleet's steaming range, and the time it could stay at sea, depended on the distance from the nearest coaling base when fuel stocks on board began to run low.

▽ The usually spotless decks of the battle-cruiser *Australia* are blackened as her crew coals ship.

▷ Though exhausting, coaling ship had to be done at high speed as the fleet might have to put to sea at any moment.

◁ A Dreadnought's guns were fed with ammunition by automatic hoists, but her boiler furnaces required the ceaseless efforts of an army of shovelling stokers. As they laboured in the intense heat of the **stokeholds,** it was not uncommon for stokers to collapse and sometimes even die.

The refining of oil fuel was still a very new process in 1914, though oil was sprayed on to the coal to make a hotter fire. HMS *Dreadnought* carried 1,138 tonnes (1,120 tons) of oil – but her main fuel capacity was a maximum load of 2,946 tonnes (2,900 tons) of coal. The first ships to use oil fuel only, Britain's *Queen Elizabeth* "Super-Dreadnoughts" with their eight 15-inch (38cm) guns, did not appear until 1915.

A dirty and exhausting job, coaling ship did not end when the last sackloads had been shovelled down into the bunkers. Hours of cleaning were then needed to rid the ship of coal dust and grit. And until the time came for the next coaling, the stokers below toiled like miners, shovelling coal from bunker to bunker to keep the load level and make sure that the ship stayed on an even keel.

"All guns load"

The men who crewed the gun turrets of a Dreadnought – those who were responsible for loading and firing the guns – were only the last handful in a long chain of hard-working teams. This chain stretched below the turret via a series of working chambers to the **magazine** below the waterline, which held the ammunition for each turret. The total number of crew of each turret, from magazine to gun crew, came to nearly 100 officers and men.

The supreme danger to all of them was the cordite explosive used to propel the shells. This was passed upward from the magazine to the guns by a series of hoists, with each shell being followed into the turret by its cordite **charge**.

If an enemy shell burst into the turret and set alight a waiting cordite charge the enormous flare of the burning cordite would do more than instantly kill the gun crew. It would flash downward into the chamber below and set off the cordite charges there, and so on downwards until

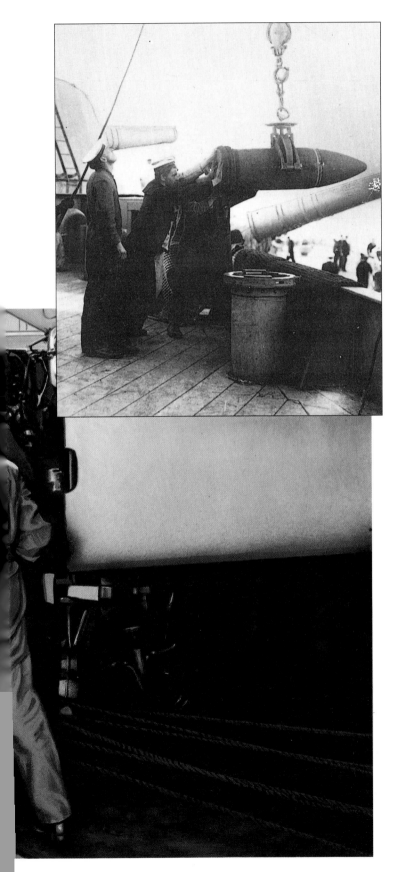

the magazine area was reached. Unless the magazine could be flooded in time, the whole ship would blow up – as happened to three British ships at the Battle of Jutland (31 May 1916).

The gun and turret crews wore white **anti-flash gear.** The hoods and gloves were some protection against cordite flash, but their post of duty was one of the most dangerous in the ship. Only months of discipline and training could keep the ammunition flowing smoothly upwards to the guns, and keep the guns firing at their best possible rate of fire.

Hydraulic rammers thrust the shell and its charge into the gun. The heavy **breech** was then closed and given a half-turn to lock its screw threads tight against the coming blast of the charge. Only then was a device called an interceptor closed to set the "Gun Ready" lamp burning in the ship's central Transmitting Station. Then the command "Shoot!" was given to all guns by the Gunnery Officer.

Details of changes of range to the target and to the angle of elevation needed for the guns were calculated in a central director and passed to the turrets by the Transmitting Station. This method of firing the guns all together, known as 'Director Firing', had only been introduced between 1910 and the outbreak of World War I.

◁ Seamen loading one of the six-inch guns on HMS *Malaya.* Ammunition for these guns was light enough to carry.

△ ◁ What a 15-inch shell looked like. It is being hoisted aboard the "Super-Dreadnought" HMS *Queen Elizabeth,* which carried eight 15-inch guns in twin turrets.

Death of a U-Boat

Although it was a mighty floating weapon of destruction, the Dreadnought battleship had one supreme foe. This was the latest form of warship to be developed by 1914: the submarine – able to stalk its prey unseen below the surface and attack with torpedoes. The torpedo, striking below the waterline and the victim's armoured **belt**, could sink even the strongest battleship. It was for this reason that battleships were fitted with anti-torpedo nets carried on long spars or booms, which could be swung out from the ship's sides to protect against torpedo attack when at anchor. But these nets could not be used when the battleship was at sea.

The British went to war in 1914 with 29 Dreadnoughts against the 20 of Germany – but this apparent lead was never viewed as a safe one. If exposed to attacks by German submarines or U-boats (short for *Unterseeboote*), the British battle fleet could easily be cut down to a strength which the German battle fleet could tackle on equal terms. For this reason the British Dreadnought "Grand Fleet" was based at the lonely anchorage of Scapa Flow in the Orkney Islands, at the extreme range of U-boats sailing from Germany.

The wisdom of this move was proved by an early success by the U-boat fleet. On 22 September 1914, three old British cruisers were sunk within minutes of each other by the submarine *U-9*, with the loss of 1,459 officers and men, out of 2,200.

On 18 March 1915, the British got their revenge when *U-29* tried to attack a British Dreadnought force exercising in the North Sea. The U-boat's torpedo missed the battleship *Neptune*, and the submarine's periscope was sighted by an alert lookout in *Dreadnought*. The huge battleship swung out of line and raced in to attack before the U-boat could dive to a safe depth. Rammed fair and square by *Dreadnought*, *U-29* was sunk within seconds. There were no survivors.

▷ The ramming and sinking of *U-29* by *Dreadnought* on 18 March 1915 was the only time, in either of the two World Wars, when a battleship managed to destroy an enemy submarine in a ramming attack. Usually the mere threat of enemy submarines caused battleships to retreat out of range of their torpedoes. But thanks to a lookout's sharp eyes, there was no escape for *U-29* and her crew on 18 March 1915.

Mines!

U-boats and their torpedoes were not the only undersea weapons feared by the crew of Dreadnought battleships. Just as deadly was the mine: a drifting or anchored explosive charge which was dropped in the sea by an enemy ship or submarine, in an area where ships were likely to run into it. Mines work like torpedoes, causing immense damage by exploding against the unarmoured part of a ship below the waterline.

By 1914 the mine was a well-known weapon in war at sea. Mines had been used with great effect in the Crimean War (1854-6), the American Civil War (1861-5), and in the most recent sea war between battleship navies: the war between Russia and Japan of 1904–5.

When World War I began, the knowledge that Germany had put down dense fields of mines to protect its harbours caused the British to refuse to risk sailing Dreadnoughts too close to the German coast. But Britain soon learned that the Germans could lay mines in British waters too. On 27 October 1914, the first Dreadnought battleship of the war was lost without having fired a shot – sunk by a mine.

It happened during the nervous early months of the war, when the British were trying to make the new Grand Fleet base at Scapa Flow safe from U-boat attack. Until this had been done, by laying dense belts of mines, the Grand Fleet had to stay in Scottish and Northern Irish

△ The crew of HMS *Audacious* takes to the lifeboats. The standard weight of this Dreadnought was 23,000 tons, was protected by 12 inches (30.5cm) of armour plate and carried ten 13.5-inch guns. A single German mine ripped her open and sank her.

waters. Here, it was thought, the battleships would be safe from surprise attack. The sinking of a Dreadnought by a mine in British waters came as a tremendous shock.

The victim was HMS *Audacious*, a powerful Dreadnought of the *King George V* class, armed with ten 13.5-inch (34.3cm) guns. While based at Lough Swilly in Northern Ireland, *Audacious* sailed with the rest of her battle squadron to carry out gunnery practice at sea. The mine hit by *Audacious* on the morning of 27 October exploded beside one of her engine rooms, causing severe flooding which made the ship heel over.

The damage should not have been fatal. Like all big ships, *Audacious* was divided into watertight compartments. Attempts were made to restore the ship to an even keel by flooding watertight compartments on the side of the ship away from the damage. Only after this was done was it found that many of the compartments were not watertight at all, and the flooding rapidly got out of control. Rough seas made it impossible to tow *Audacious* back to harbour, and after nearly twelve hours she blew up and sank. Happily, all her complement of 782 officers and men were saved first.

The long vigil

For nearly two years, the rival Dreadnought fleets of Britain and Germany warily faced each other across the North Sea – the British from the Grand Fleet base at Scapa Flow, the Germans from the base of their "High Seas Fleet" at Wilhelmshaven.

Outnumbered as they were, the Germans had no intention of risking a massive fleet battle that could wipe them out at a stroke. They hoped to ambush a part of the British fleet before help could come to its aid and crush it with their main fleet, thereby gradually cutting down the British Dreadnought strength to that of Germany.

For their part, the British tried repeatedly to send out small forces which would make the main strength of the German fleet attack – and run straight into a British ambush. From time to time, both fleets would make a "sweep" into the North Sea, each side hoping to bring on the sort of battle it wanted. But by the New Year of 1916 it was beginning to seem that "The Day" would never come when the rival fleets would meet in battle.

During this weary waiting game, life was far harder for the British sailors than for the Germans. The crews of the High Seas Fleet in Wilhelmshaven did not have to live day in, day out, aboard their ships; instead they lived in comfortable barracks ashore, able to man their ships at very short notice. But the British sailors, up at Scapa Flow in the desolate Orkney Islands, had no choice but to live aboard their ships for months at a time before going home on leave. Nowadays they would have movies, video, TV and radio – but during World War I there were none of these things, and men cooped up aboard ship had to make their own entertainment when off duty.

This they did with a spirit that often astonished their officers. Each ship had its own star musicians, bands, comedians, and concert parties – but the main outlet during the long months of boredom was sport. Ashore there was inter-ship boxing, cricket and football, and all of them were keenly contested.

A most useful blend of sporting

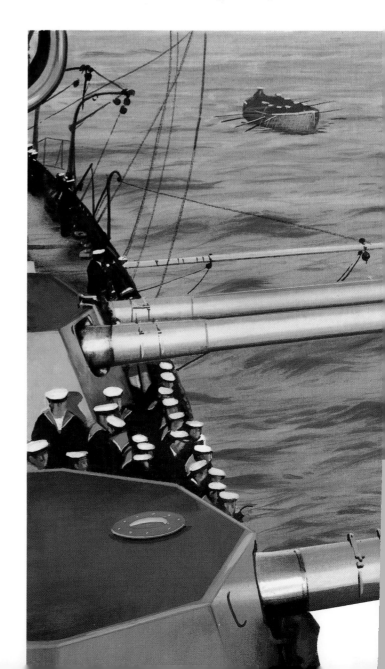

competition and routine naval training was the fleet regatta: boat races between the crews of the ships' cutters. This was a very tiring but, at the same time, most effective way of working off surplus energy, with the prize of a cup being offered for the best crew in the fleet.

▽ Cheered on by their shipmates, three cutter crews battle for the prize of a cup in a fleet regatta in Scapa Flow — one of the best ways of keeping the men fit during the weary months of waiting for the German Fleet to come out.

The Grand Fleet deploys

"The Day" came at last on 31 May 1916: the long-awaited clash of the British and German Dreadnought fleets remembered as the Battle of Jutland.

The battle began with the decision of the German Admiral Reinhard Scheer to take the High Seas Fleet to sea in the hope of ambushing the British Grand Fleet's heavy scouting force: the fast, heavily armed yet lightly armoured Dreadnought battle-cruisers commanded by Admiral David Beatty. What Scheer did not know was that the British in London had learned how to "listen in" to German radio signals as the High Seas Fleet prepared to put to sea. As a result, the British Admiral John

Jellicoe, commanding the Grand Fleet's Dreadnought battleships at Scapa Flow, was given the chance he had been waiting for since the beginning of the war: the chance to bring the entire High Seas Fleet to battle.

Jellicoe's plan was to use Beatty's battle-cruisers as bait. They were to rush south, get sighted by the High Seas Fleet, then turn and run to the north – luring the High Seas Fleet within range of the Grand Fleet's battleships. To prevent Beatty's force being smashed before it could get out of range of the High Seas Fleet, the British battle-cruisers would be supported by the five *Queen Elizabeth* "Super-Dreadnought" fast battleships

▽ Vice Admiral Reinhard Scheer (right), Commander of the German Fleet, and Admiral Sir John Jellicoe (left), Commander of the British Grand Fleet in the Battle of Jutland.

▷ The spotter seaplane of HMS *Engadine* looks down on the thrilling sight of the British battle-cruiser force steaming into action in the opening phase of the Battle of Jutland.

with their speed of 24 knots, massive armour, oil-fired turbines, and the extremely powerful armament of eight 15-inch (38cm) guns each.

By the early afternoon of 31 May Jellicoe's plan seemed to have every chance of success. Scouting ships had made contact with the on-coming High Seas Fleet, and Beatty's force was about to join battle with the German battle-cruisers scouting ahead of the High Seas Fleet's battleships. Up above a floatplane from the seaplane carrier *Engadine* looked down on the awesome sight of a battle fleet steaming into action in "line-ahead", looming through the pearly mist of the May afternoon.

"Equal Speed Charlie London"

The fight between the British and German battlecruisers which began the Battle of Jutland did not go well for the British. *Indefatigable* and *Queen Mary* blew up and sank after cordite flash fires from German hits reached their magazines. The same thing nearly happened to Beatty's flagship *Lion* after one of her turrets was hit, but the turret commander saved the ship by bravely giving the order to flood the magazine before he died.

For all that, the opening phase of the battle had done what Jellicoe wanted. Beatty had sighted the 22 battleships of the High Seas Fleet and had turned north, luring the Germans towards the British battleships led by Jellicoe. But nothing else was clear. Beatty's position was uncertain, and so was that of the Germans. To use the big guns of his fleet to best advantage, Jellicoe had to decide in which direction to turn his fleet.

The Grand Fleet's battleships steamed south in six parallel columns, and it was up to Jellicoe whether to order them to go into line-ahead to the left or right. The wrong decision could easily leave his ships still turning into "line-ahead" as they came under fire from the German

▽ The German High Seas Fleet steams forward on the morning of the Battle of Jutland, 31 May 1916.

guns. This would have been a certain recipe for disaster.

It was a decision which Jellicoe would never have had to make if his scouting forces had given him the right information. As he peered into the deepening mist (made worse by funnel smoke) the decision was his, and his alone. Finally he spoke to his signals officer, ordering him to signal the fleet to turn to the south-east with all ships making the same speed.

At Trafalgar in 1805, Nelson had sent his ships into battle with the famous signal: "ENGLAND EXPECTS THAT EVERY MAN WILL DO HIS DUTY". Jellicoe's signal at Jutland was "EQUAL SPEED CHARLIE LONDON".

▽ Throughout most of the battle, mist and dense funnel smoke made it hard for the fleets to see each other.

▷ Up the signal **halyards** of HMS *Iron Duke,* runs the historic flag hoist: "EQUAL SPEED CHARLIE LONDON."

British "Grand Fleet"

How the fleets deployed at Jutland.

German "High Seas Fleet"

Torpedoes approaching

Though Jellicoe's decision on turning his fleet proved to be correct, Admiral Scheer surprised him twice. The German line of battleships came looming out of the mist to find the dim horizon ahead ablaze with an unbroken line of thundering British guns – but Scheer swiftly turned his fleet and retreated.

Now the battle became a matter of Jellicoe trying to cut off the way home for the Germans, and Scheer trying to find a way round the line of British guns. As the fleets closed on each other once more, Scheer ordered his destroyers to charge the British line and make the one attack which battleships dared not ignore: an attack with torpedoes.

Before Admiral Fisher had introduced the Dreadnought with its "all big-gun" design, battleships had carried a wide range of guns for precisely this moment. The idea had been to keep firing at the enemy battleships with the heaviest guns, while the lighter guns concentrated on fighting off the threat of torpedo-carrying ships. But by the time of the Battle of Jutland, fear of the mere threat of a torpedo attack meant that even the most powerful battleships had only one answer to approaching torpedo craft. This was to turn away out of range, leaving the smallest possible target to the approaching torpedoes.

To make quite sure of saving his battleships, Scheer also ordered the German battle-cruisers to make what became known as a "death-ride" against the British line – a head-on charge in which the German ships suffered terrible punishment.

▷ The sight most dreaded by even the most powerful battleship: the bubbling tracks of approaching torpedoes, made by the compressed air driving the missiles rising to the surface.

This was the most dramatic moment of the Battle of Jutland, which robbed the British of their last chance to overwhelm the High Seas Fleet in a decisive battle.

It was during the "death-ride" of the German battle-cruisers that their flagship *Lützow* suffered such extensive damage that she later had to be abandoned and sunk. But the instinctive turn-away by Jellicoe and Beatty from the threat of the German torpedo attack enabled Scheer to reverse his fleet for the second time and escape out of range of the British battleships. Under cover of darkness, daringly steering through the rear line of the British Grand Fleet, Scheer led his fleet safely back to Wilhelmshaven.

The biggest broadside

Perhaps the strangest story of all the ships that fought at Jutland was that of HMS *Agincourt*. Though British-built, she had not been built for the British Navy at all. She had been built at the Armstrong yard on the River Tyne, and from the start she was a status symbol: the battleship with the largest number of guns in the world.

She was ordered by Brazil before World War I as the *Rio de Janeiro* to be the pride of the Brazilian Navy in that country's struggle for naval supremacy with Chile and Argentina. Brazil wanted *Rio de Janeiro* to be even bigger than the two battleships she had ordered in 1907: *Minas Geraes* and *Sao Paolo*, both with twelve 12-inch guns. *Rio de Janeiro* was designed to carry fourteen 12-inch guns, more than any other battleship afloat, and she was also the longest battleship in the world – 192.6 metres (632 ft), compared with the 149.3 metres (490 ft) of HMS *Dreadnought*.

But *Rio de Janeiro* never served with the Brazilian Navy. Before she was completed, the Brazilian Government ran out of money to pay for her, and the huge ship was bought by Turkey as the *Sultan Osman I*. Then in the summer of 1914, when it became clear that Turkey would fight on Germany's side, she was taken over by the British. The battleship was completed and added to the Grand Fleet.

"The Giant" as she had been called by the workers who built her on Tyneside, joined the Grand Fleet as HMS *Agincourt*. From the luxury of her fittings and the unusually generous space of her living quarters, *Agincourt* was known in the Fleet as the "Gin Palace". A legend grew that *Agincourt* was the only battleship in the world which never dare fire all her guns in a full broadside, because there were so many of them she would break her back. But this myth was triumphantly disproved in the Battle of Jutland, when *Agincourt* repeatedly hurled full broadsides at the German fleet – though the terrific shock of the guns left hardly an intact cup or plate in the ship!

◁ Known as the "Gin Palace" in the British Grand Fleet because of the luxurious fittings ordered by her previous Brazilian and Turkish owners, HMS *Agincourt* opens fire at Jutland with her awesome broadside of fourteen 12-inch guns.

▽ Unlike the British battle-cruisers, those of the German High Seas Fleet stood up well to the pounding of heavy shells. This is how the German battle-cruiser *Seydlitz* looked in **dry dock** after struggling home from the Battle of Jutland.

The High Seas Fleet surrenders

The Battle of Jutland was an enormous disappointment for the British Navy. The German fleet had not only escaped from the long-awaited battle but had lost fewer ships than the British: one battle-cruiser and one old battleship, against three British battle-cruisers.

Jutland was the last big sea battle of World War I. The High Seas Fleet never again risked so dangerous a trial of strength. Although both fleets continued to make occasional "sweeps" in the North Sea, they never met in battle again.

The next time the fleets saw each other was after Germany had surrendered (11 November 1918). Part of the terms for Germany's surrender was that she must give up her battle fleet in a formal naval surrender, which was made at sea on 21 November 1918.

Until the very last moment, the British could not believe that the German fleet would tamely surrender without a last

◁ Ready for action in their anti-flash gear, men of the Grand Fleet crowd the rails as the German Fleet surrenders.

fight. With their American allies, the Grand Fleet lay waiting to receive the surrender of the High Seas Fleet – in two enormous lines of British battleships 12 kilometres (7.5 miles) long. All ships were at battle stations, with their guns loaded.

As the silent German warships steamed between the Allied lines, the sailors of the British and American fleets crowded the rails to watch. After so many years of patient waiting, it was hard to believe that the war of the Dreadnoughts was ending without a shot being fired.

But the Germans had no intention of letting the Allies take over their ships. After months of captivity in Scapa Flow, the crews opened the sea-cocks of their great ships. The water flooded in, and on 21 June 1919, they sank into the water whilst still at anchor.

▽ The scene in Scapa Flow before the German High Seas Fleet sank itself by **scuttling**, on 21 June 1919.

▷ Only the funnels and upperworks of the German battleship *Hindenburg* remain above water after the scuttling.

Glossary

Anti-flash gear White protective clothing for head and arms, worn to reduce risk of injury from burns.

Armour plate Plates of toughened steel to defend a ship against an explosive shell.

Battle-cruiser Larger and faster than a battleship, armed with battleship-sized guns, but lacking the heavy armour of the true battleship.

▽ The North Sea battleground of the British and German Dreadnought navies, showing the converging of the fleets and the area where the Battle of Jutland was fought on 31 May 1916.

Belt The armoured protection along a ship's sides.

Breech The end of a gun through which the shell and charge are loaded; it is locked shut before the gun is fired.

Broadside The maximum number of guns of the same size that a ship can fire.

Charge Cylindrical portion of explosive (usually cordite) used to fire a shell.

Deadlight Metal-plated shutter hinged inboard above a scuttle to guard against storms and block out light in battle.

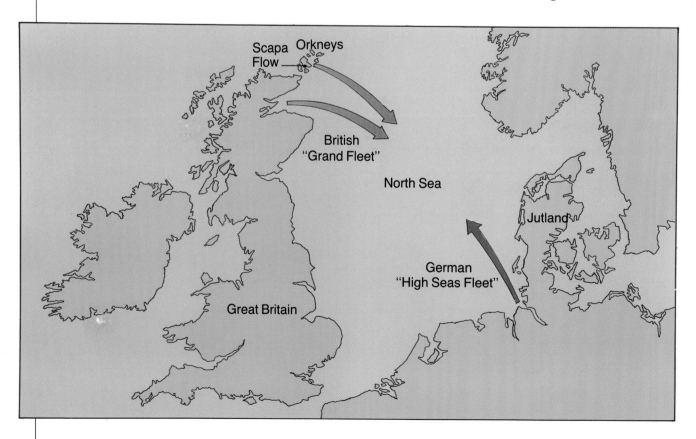

Timechart

Dreadnought General term for a battleship armed with more than six heavy guns and capable of steaming at over 20 knots.

Dry dock Dock that can be drained of water to allow a ship to be examined and repaired.

Halyard Light rope used for hoisting sails or flags.

Magazine Hold for storing explosive charges.

Mess-deck A crew's living quarters aboard ship.

Scuttle, to Sink one's own ship by blowing holes in its sides or opening its valves to the sea.

Scuttles Round portholes in a ship's side to admit air and light.

Squadron A group of warships forming part of a fleet.

Stokehold The working area where stokers feed a ship's furnaces with fuel.

Tripod mast Mast of three heavy struts – distinguishing mark of a Dreadnought battleship or battle-cruiser.

Turret Armoured enclosure for a ship's guns.

1805 (21 October) Battle of Trafalgar: last large-scale fleet battle on the open sea before Jutland.
1859 France produces the first armour-plated warship (*Gloire*).
1860 Britain produces the first iron-built armoured warship (*Warrior*).
1862 First gun battle between armoured warships (*Merrimack* and *Monitor*, in American Civil War).
1872 Britain produces the first turret-gun battleship entirely lacking masts and sails (HMS *Devastation*).
1906 Britain launches the first Dreadnought battleship (HMS *Dreadnought*).
1907 Britain launches the first Dreadnought battle-cruiser (HMS *Invincible*).
1908 First German Dreadnought battleship and battle-cruiser are launched (*Rheinland* and *Von der Tann*).
1914 (August) Outbreak of World War I. Britain's Grand Fleet of Dreadnoughts moves to its war base at Scapa Flow.
1915 (24 January) German battle-cruisers escape British battle-cruisers in Battle of the Dogger Bank.
1915 (18 March) HMS *Dreadnought* rams and sinks German submarine *U-29*.
1916 (31 May) Battle of Jutland.
1918 (21 November) German High Seas Fleet surrenders at sea.
1919 (21 June) High Seas Fleet scuttles itself in Scapa Flow.

Index

PRINTED IN BELGIUM BY

INTERNATIONAL BOOK PRODUCTION